MICHAEL JACKSON
Instrumental Solos

CONTENTS

Arranged by BILL GALLIFORD, ETHAN NEUBURG and TOD EDMONDSON

Produced by
Alfred Music Publishing Co., Inc.
P.O. Box 10003
Van Nuys, CA 91410-0003
alfred.com

Printed in USA.

ISBN-10: 0-7390-7802-X
ISBN-13: 978-0-7390-7802-0

 Alfred Cares. Contents printed on 100% recycled paper.

Track 1: Demo

BEAT IT

Written and Composed by
MICHAEL JACKSON

Moderately fast ♩ = 138

Verse:

4

BILLIE JEAN

Track 2: Demo

Written and Composed by
MICHAEL JACKSON

Billie Jean - 5 - 1

Chorus:

10

Billie Jean - 5 - 5

BLACK OR WHITE

Rap Lyrics Written by
BILL BOTTRELL

Written and Composed by
MICHAEL JACKSON

Track 3: Demo

Black or White - 5 - 1

Optional Rap:

33

(Spoken:) Protection for gangs, clubs, and nations, causing grief in human relations.

It's a turf war, on a global scale. I'd rather hear both sides of the tale.

You see, it's not about races, just places,   *faces. Where your blood comes from is where your space is.*

I've seen the sharp get duller,   *I'm not going to spend my life being a color.*

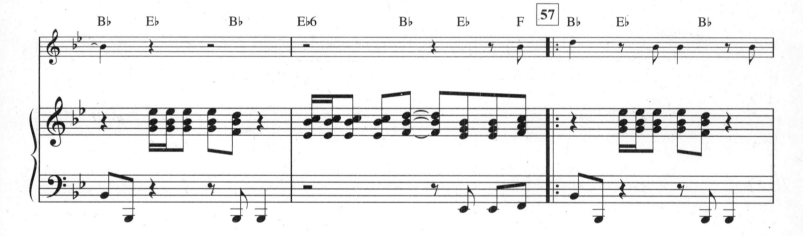

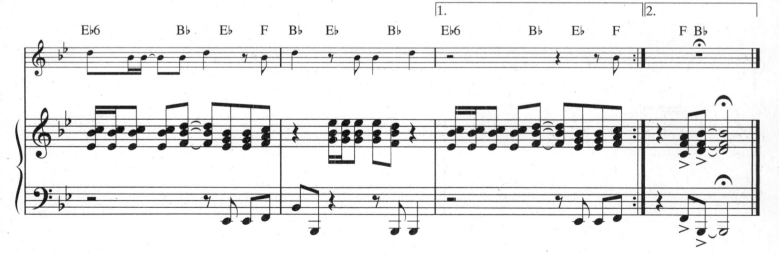

DON'T STOP 'TIL YOU GET ENOUGH

Track 4: Demo

Written and Composed by
MICHAEL JACKSON

Moderate dance tempo ♩ = 112

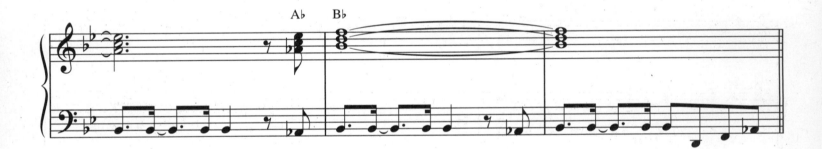

Verse:

Don't Stop 'til You Get Enough - 5 - 1

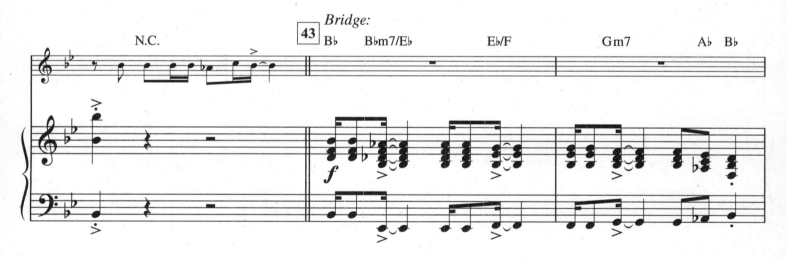

Chorus:

HUMAN NATURE

Track 5: Demo

Words and Music by
JOHN BETTIS and JEFF PORCARO

Human Nature - 5 - 1

To Coda ⊕ |1.

|2.

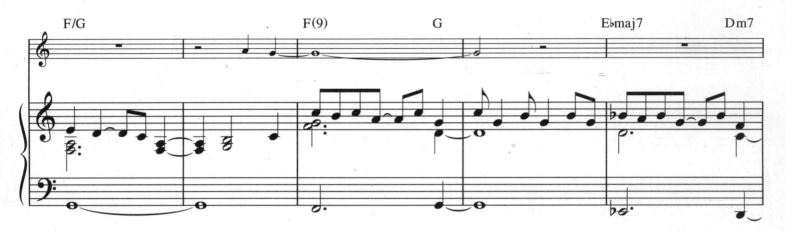

D.S. ℅ al Coda

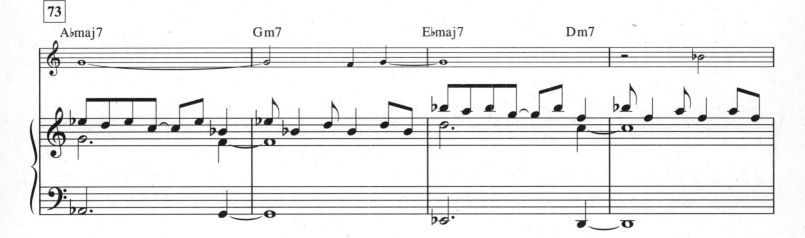

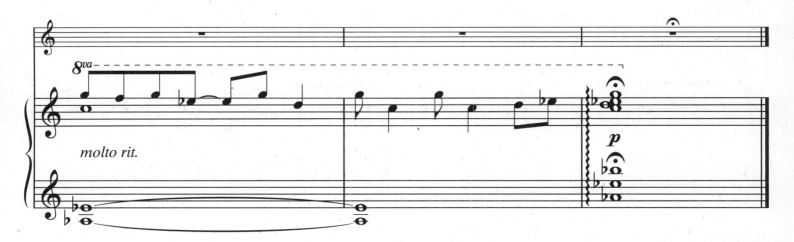

I JUST CAN'T STOP LOVING YOU

Track 6: Demo

Written and Composed by
MICHAEL JACKSON

I Just Can't Stop Loving You - 4 - 1

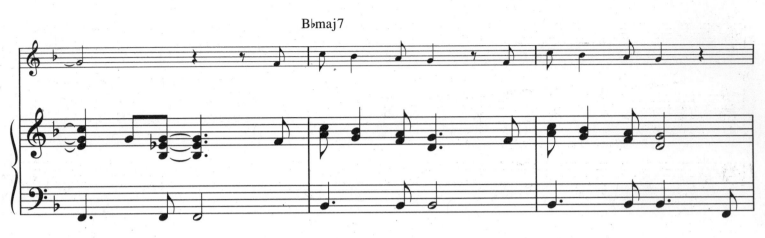

I Just Can't Stop Loving You - 4 - 4

THE WAY YOU MAKE ME FEEL

Track 7: Demo

Written and Composed by
MICHAEL JACKSON

Moderate shuffle rock ♩. = 112

N.C.

The Way You Make Me Feel - 5 - 1

Verse:

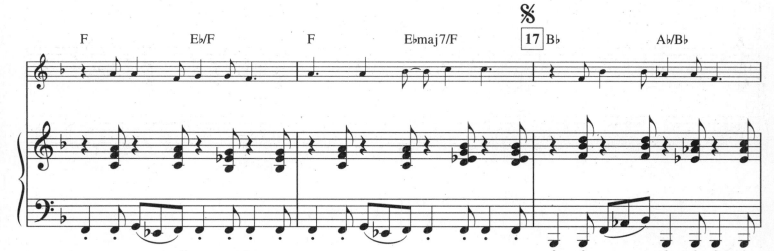

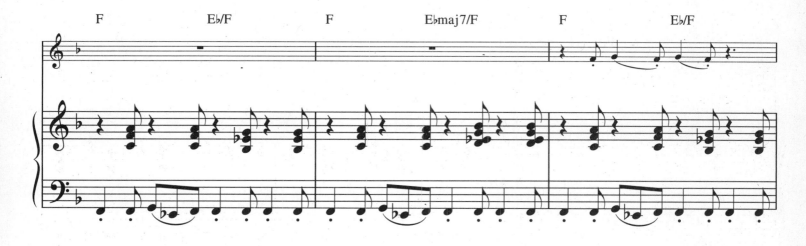

The Way You Make Me Feel - 5 - 4

SHE'S OUT OF MY LIFE

Track 8: Demo

Words and Music by
TOM BAHLER

She's Out of My Life - 3 - 1

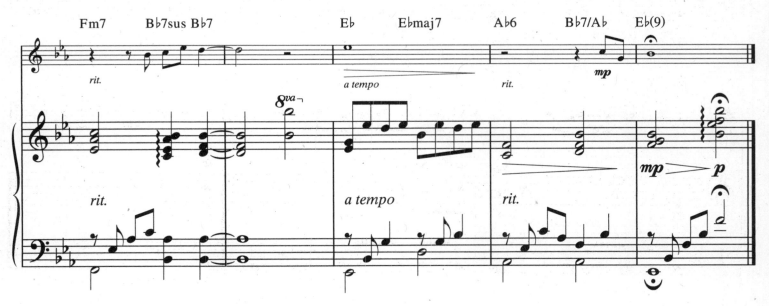

She's Out of My Life - 3 - 3

WILL YOU BE THERE

Track 9: Demo

Written and Composed by
MICHAEL JACKSON

Moderate gospel feel (♩ = 80)

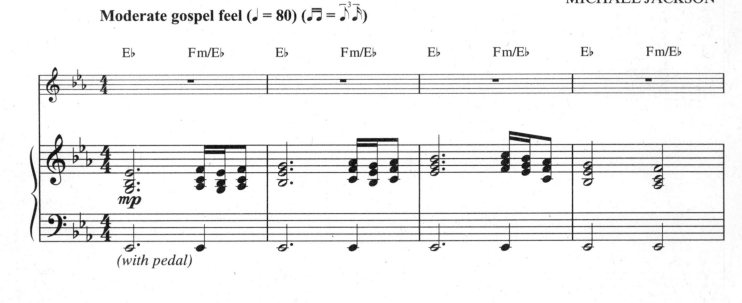

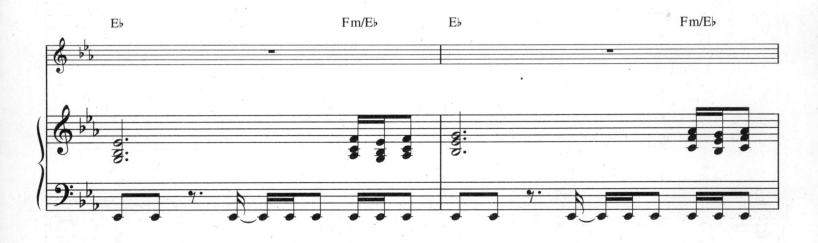

Will You Be There - 5 - 1

Verse:

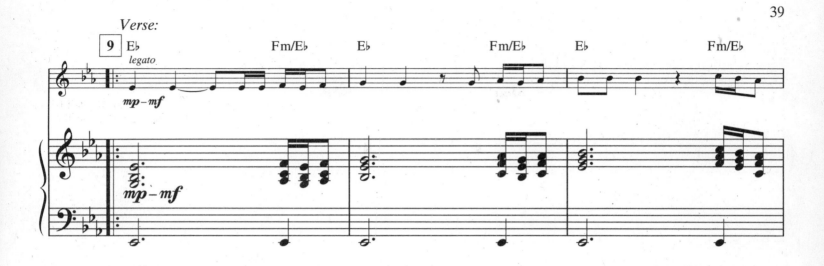

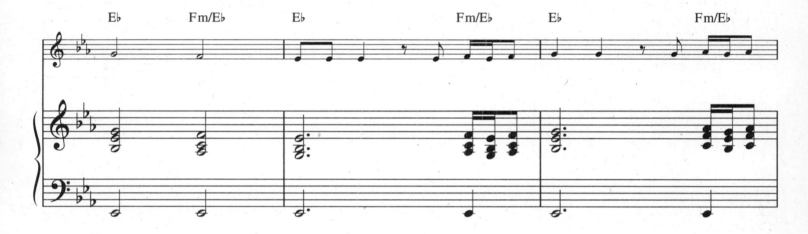

MAN IN THE MIRROR

Words and Music by
SIEDAH GARRETT and GLEN BALLARD

Track 10: Demo

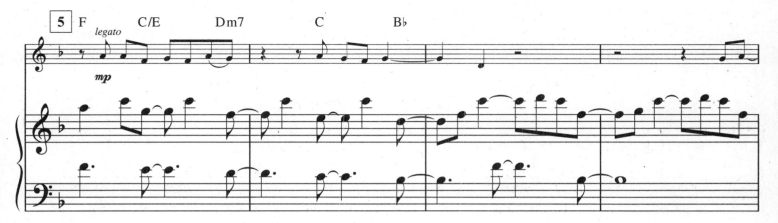

Verse:

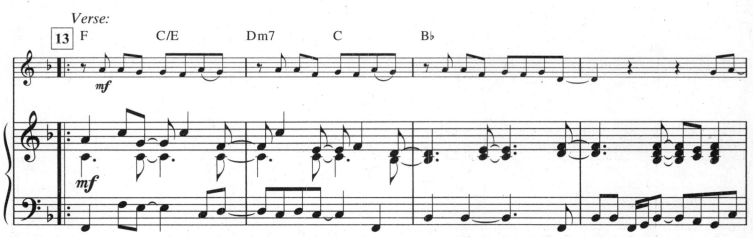

Man in the Mirror - 3 - 1

Track 11: Demo

THRILLER

Words and Music by
ROD TEMPERTON

Moderate R&B rock ♩ = 108

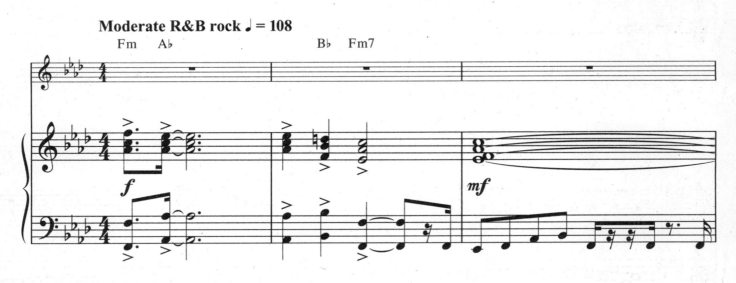

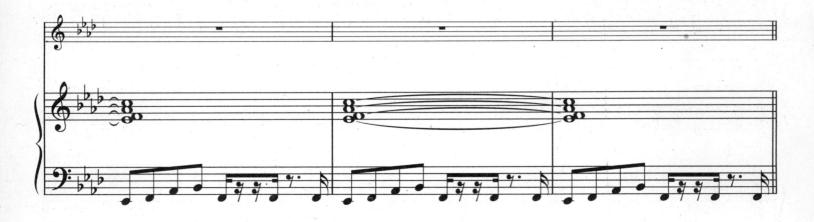

Thriller - 5 - 1

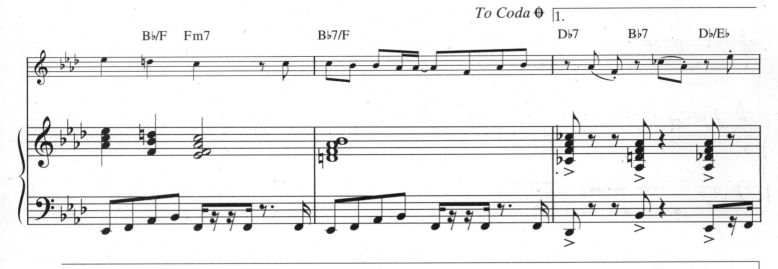

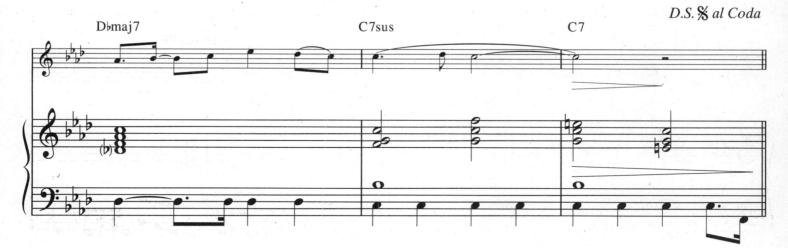

⊕ Coda

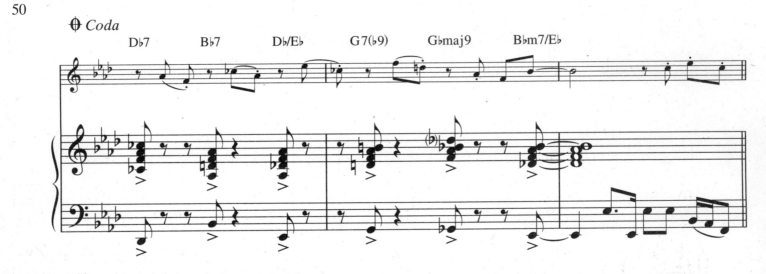

Chorus:

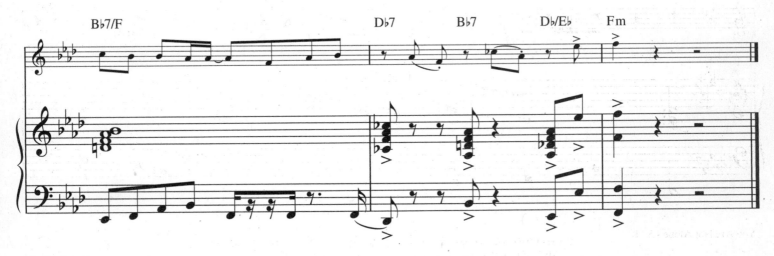

YOU ARE NOT ALONE

Words and Music by
R. KELLY

Slowly ♩ = 60

Verse:

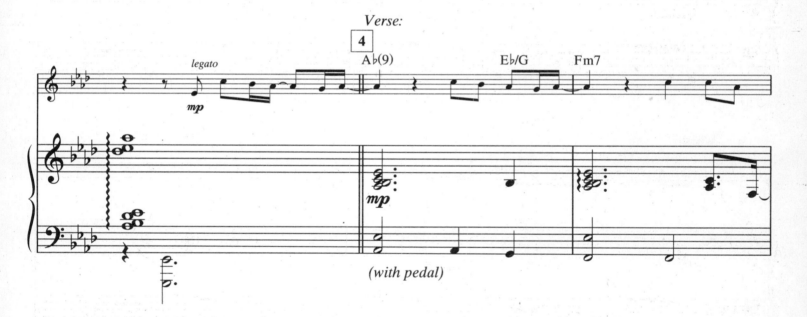

(with pedal)

You Are Not Alone - 5 - 1

54

Chorus:

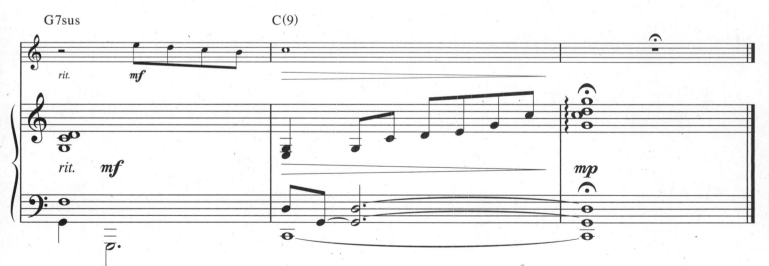

You Are Not Alone - 5 - 5

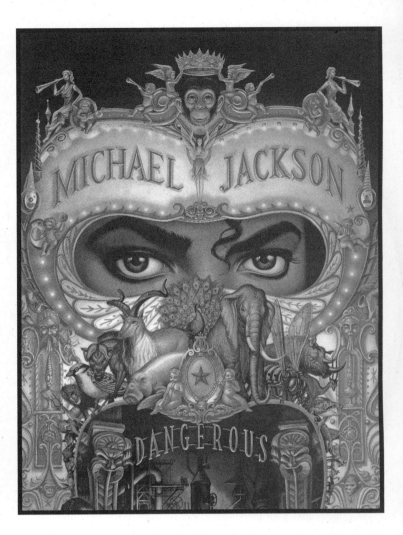

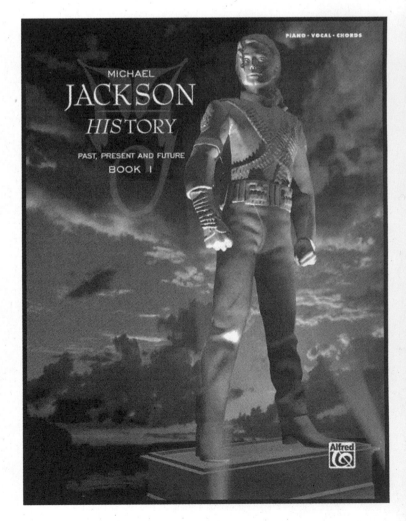